Bully ME? ...Oh No!!!

A Resource for Teens to know ...Suicide is not an option

By Patrice Lee

Copyright 2013
Published by Feinstein & Associates d/b/a Leep4Joy Bks
Printed in the United States of America

Publisher's Cataloging-In-Publication Data
(Prepared by The Donohue Group, Inc.)

Names: Lee, Patrice.
Title: Bully me? ... Oh no!!! : a resource for teens to know ... suicide is not an option / by Patrice Lee.
Description: Oak Park, MI : Feinstein & Associates d/b/a Leep4Joy Bks, [2013] | Interest age level: 12 and up. | Summary: "A teen resource on bully prevention to help teens understand that bullying is not okay, and suicide is not an option. The reader will see how the author turns an embarrassing bully moment into an unforgettable laughing experience. More than 200 encouraging words to build self-esteem and encourage self-respect, anti-bully pledge, more ..."--Provided by publisher.
Identifiers: ISBN 9780983720737 | ISBN 9780986316791 (ebook)
Subjects: LCSH: Bullying--Prevention--Juvenile literature. | Teenagers--Suicidal behavior--Juvenile literature. | Self-esteem in adolescence--Juvenile literature. | CYAC: Bullying--Prevention. | Teenagers--Suicidal behavior. | Self-esteem in adolescence.
Classification: LCC BF637.B85 L44 2013 (print) | LCC BF637.B85 (ebook) | DDC 302.343--dc23

All rights reserved. This publication may not be reproduced or transmitted in any form, electronically, by photocopy or recording, without prior written consent of the publisher.

Edited by: Mary Edwards, Cathryn Williams
Cover Art: Bob Ivory, Jr., Ivory Coast Media

Send all correspondence to: Leep4Joy Books, P.O. Box 48172, Oak Park, MI 48237

Bully Me. . .Oh NO!!!

Dedication

This book is dedicated to every teenager, youth or young adult who has contemplated suicide in their lifetime. Know that our Heavenly Father loves you immensely, more than you'll ever know. May you find comfort, gain strength, and experience healing from this resource on your journey to become whole. You are loved with an everlasting love, and always know that someone is concerned about you.

Bully Me. . .Oh NO!!!

Bully Me...Oh NO!!!

Table of Contents

	Endorsement	9
	Foreword	11
	Introduction	15
I.	Please Hold On...	17
II.	A Mirror Image	31
III.	Living with Great Expectation (For a Great Life)	43
IV.	Power Play	49
V.	A Work in Progress	63
VI.	Bully Tips	73
VII.	LAUGH!!! ...and LOL	83
VIII.	The Stats	93
IX.	"Fear" Not!	97
X.	Life Changing Words (For a Better Life)	107
XI.	TEEN Strategy and Review	115

Bully Me. . .Oh NO!!!

Endorsements

"Bully Me? …Oh NO!!!" by Patrice Lee, is a thoughtful, hands on approach for teens who are dealing with bullying. She educates her young readers with grace and humor, helping teens reach the powerful potential that comes with developing self-respect as well as respect for others. But, *"Bully Me? …Oh NO!!!,"* is not just for teens, it for teachers who work with young people as well, and is a great resource for the entire family to read together.
~ **Brenda High** – Founder, Bully Police USA

www.bullypolice.com

The *"Bully ME? . . ."* books are a part of a series whose time has come. Patrice Lee zeros in on the key issues surrounding modern day bullying. As an experienced school administrator and youth minister, I know that Patrice is in tune and on time with her approach and topical advice.

Jonathan M. Wynne, M.A., M.B.A.
Dean of Students, Henry Ford Academy H. S.

Bully Me. . .Oh NO!!!

"Three days after I gave my daughter your Teen Resource, '*Bully Me? ...Oh No!!!*' she came to me and said, 'Mom! <u>Thank you for this book. You didn't know it, but, I was thinking about suicide. This book changed my life</u>." (It was a total shock to this Mom, for happily shared at the time of purchase that she talked to her girls every day.)

Delshawnna M., Working mom, Michigan

"We commend Ms. Lee for her insight and wisdom as it relates to the bullying concerns in our society. Because of her personal experiences, her books will help us in our endeavors to rid our communities of bullies. Her work is beneficial for churches, schools, and community organizations, as well as individual families." May God bless your work.

Michael and Theresa Searcy,
President/Director, Searcy Community Center

"The message you are sending to children and parents plays a very important role in forming a better functioning society of young leaders, doctors, conscious thinkers, etc., who will play crucial roles in future societies. Thanks for being such a strong trailblazer!"

S. Scott, Youngstown, Ohio

Bully Me...Oh NO!!!

Foreword
By Dr. Sabrina Jackson, Clinical Therapist
"The People Expert"

Bullying has become a household word in our schools, in the media, at church and in the legislature. One of the main reasons for the increased discussion is that the effects of bullying have become fatal among our youth and children.

As a child growing up, I experienced bullying because I was a very dark-skinned child. Students would call me "Tar Baby," "Blackie," and other derogatory names. When I became a pre-teen, the situation got worse since my name is Sabrina. Then I became "Sabrina-The-Teen-Age-Witch." And sometimes my classmates changed the "W" in witch to a "B."

Although things were bad, I never felt like they were completely hopeless. However, my self-esteem waived for years until 9th grade. You see there was this "fine" football player named Stan in my high school. In my eyes, Stan was the "The Man," but I never thought he would look at me, since I was a freshman and dark-skinned.

Well, one day as Stan walked past me in the hallway, he said, "Hey, dark and lovely." Wow!!

Bully Me...Oh NO!!!

That changed something within me, and I began to embrace my skin color, so much so, that I put that phrase on my t-shirts, jeans and jackets.

Today, however, many youth feel that things will never get better for them and that there's no reason to live. They allow their feelings to dictate successful attempts at suicide. So month after month, stories of their suicides dominate major news headlines.

Such headlines read: "After years of in-school and on-line harassment, 14 year old "E" committed suicide;" and "J, age 12, experienced depression and committed suicide because of cruel treatment by his classmates;" and "F. hurled herself in front of a train after Tweeting "I can't! I'm done! I give up!"

That is why this resource for teens is so important. "Bullycides," as described above, continue to increase among teens. For that reason, I am so excited about Patrice Lee's book, which addresses the problem and offers practical advice and solutions.

"Bully Me?...Oh No!!!," . . .Suicide is not an option, is designed also to give teens hope. The message is: Yes, you may feel alone, but you are never alone because God is with you. You may feel weak, but it is in your weakness that God is strong. You may feel less-than, not liked, or even not loved, but God loves you and has a purpose of goodness for your life.

In these pages you will learn how to love yourself…..no matter how it looks, feels, or sounds; and you will know that you are loved!!!

I encourage you to read and discover that while "...*Suicide Is Not an Option*," discovering and developing your purpose, and then delivering that purpose, is a very real option when you love you!!!

(Dr. Jackson is a Clinical Therapist who is referred to, and known by many as "The People Expert.")

Bully Me. . .Oh NO!!!

Bully Me...Oh NO!!!

Introduction

In the Teen Edition, I share real stories of bully encounters that personally affected my family and me. One bully encounter involved a form of crowd bullying, another of one who suffered extreme bullying throughout the course of his life. Although the bullying was on a different scale, the illustrations stress the importance of immediate and strong, action as the best solution.

While this book is about discovering practical ways to cope with bullying, it also provides proactive measures you can take to avoid confrontation in general, in order to live a more peaceful life. This book offers answers to the silent questions that teens don't ask, and addresses some of their basic concerns.

In the Teen Edition of the "Bully Me? . . ." Book series, we will get to the root of some of the problems that many teens face every day. Once we've dealt with the root problems, causes and their effects on our teens, then we can begin to share a positive means of resolving the growing epidemic and problems of teen suicide, as it relates to bullying and other related matters.

Bully Me. . .Oh NO!!!

If you purchased this resource to find out about bullies and their motives, we purposely put it last, so we could address the most important topic first – "**YOU**." We want you to know that your life is extremely valuable, and you are more precious than the bullies and mean-spirited people who lack respect for others. **And you have options**...

I.
Please Hold On. . .

Bully Me...Oh NO!!!

Sometimes Bad Things Happen to Good People

Sometimes bad things happen to good people, and the act of bullying is a bad thing. Born premature at birth, he weighed in the balances between life and death for quite a duration.

This beautiful baby boy survived, but with medical conditions that would follow him for the rest of his life. Despite his health issues, this little guy approached life with the heart of a champion.

The son of two loving parents, QII also strived to do good and was a peacemaker to those who knew him. But his lot in life was one of endurance, for he was laughed at, teased, and taunted by his classmates and peers for the way he looked, throughout most of his childhood and adolescence.

This champion had many sad and lonesome moments, for he shared his pain with no one. He didn't fight back. He was simply following the example his parents had set, so he held his peace when the crowds (classmates) bullied him.

At home with his siblings, he was thoughtful, loving and kind. He loved to play games. And he loved to laugh. QII was always the first to apologize or ask forgiveness from his brother and sister whenever he had a disagreement with them. But all of those things that made him happy gradually went away.

QII endured his most severe bully attack at church in his teen years, as the physical attack he received there left him disfigured. Yet, he overcame it. Although, his parents took immediate action, and attended to his medical needs, the other parents were in denial of their son's – the bully's - actions against QII. They dismissed the matter and went on with life.

As a young man in his twenties, and after the death of his rock, our Mom, and later our Dad, all of the bullying he had endured through the years, took its' toll on him. His spirit was so broken now, that he lost the momentum to keep pushing.

QII would never regain his true zest for life. His spirit had been permanently crushed. With the walls caving in, he no longer enjoyed the quality of life he had once known. Although he never deserved to be treated with such cruelty for all of those years, he kept silent. He held it in.

He went back to work full-time after a diagnosis of clinical depression; but the guys at work took his ethical values and quiet disposition as a sign of weakness, instead of respecting his views. The taunting continued. He lost hope. And for the rest of his life he moved from facility to facility under the care or guidance of another, until his death.

Although it was painful, I shared QII's story to illustrate how bullying can affect your inner spirit. No one deserves to be constantly mistreated, for any reason, by anyone. So if you are being bullied, please speak up for yourself and get help for the bully too. Don't allow the bully's pain to cause you unnecessary grief. You don't deserve it.

I just want to say, "I love you QII. You will always be in my heart. You showed us what unconditional love was all about. You were a great brother, a champion, a true friend. My life is better because you were in it."

Bully Me...Oh NO!!!

Can You See What You've Done to Me?

Bully, can you see what you've done to me?

I was frightened and timid.
You made me feel unsure.
It became internal. I became withdrawn.

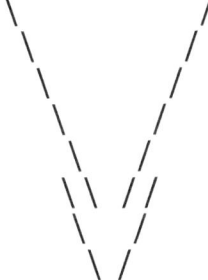

Then I decided not to let you get next to me.
I decided to hold on and just
Be strong!

Please Hold On . . .

Hold on to everything good around you. Hold on to the sanctity of life, 'cause you only get one chance to share and live out the greatness that resides within you. So, please hold on . . . to the goodness of life.

The purpose for which this book was written is to let you know that your life is a gift through your parents, to the world. You were created by Almighty God.

You are-life is-a gift; and **suicide** is not an option. I repeat, **suicide** is not, nor will it ever be an option. That means you do not have permission to take your own life.

Here's why. God is the giver of life itself. When He created you in His image, "you **were** fearfully (tremendously) **and** wonderfully (superbly, marvelously) **made.**" That means He was quite pleased (completely satisfied) when He made you. And He had a specific purpose for your life before He created you and blew into your nostrils the breath of life.

Beautiful You. There is nothing that would warrant you to take a life, especially your own. You are irreplaceable. He made you totally unique and different from others, because God is incredibly creative and likes variety. In fact, He really loves variety and all things beautiful. That's why He created beautiful you.

Have you ever witnessed a rainbow across the sky after a refreshing rain? ...The amazingly beautiful hues of the evening's sunset, or the beautiful rays across the morning sky? You can't help but notice the bursting array of color from the autumn leaves, the flowers, plant life, the foods we eat, and the thousands of beautiful fish, birds, animals and insects (butterflies)? That's variety.

He singled you out with your own set of gifts and talents to make a contribution to the world. He desires only the best of everything for you and wants to help you live a great life. He has given you a guide — His Word — to get you through any adversity that comes your way.

Imagine. You may be too young to understand the sacrifices your parents have made for you but, just imagine if you can, being responsible for the life of another human being. Imagine that you are responsible everyday for everything this person eats, where they sleep, and for their protection and safety too; and for six months you put them first on your agenda each day before tending to your needs.

Now that's a sacrifice isn't it. But, imagine how you would feel, if this person never ever showed any gratitude or stopped to say thank you.

Thank you Mom & Dad. From infancy until you are old enough to care for yourself, you have, and will depend on your parents (legal guardian) to meet all of your basic needs for the life you live today as they provide the safety and comforts of a loving home environment at no cost. They assisted you as you took your first steps, helped you say your first words and encouraged you to increase your vocabulary, as you learned to speak new words each day.

Prep Time. You learned to obey their rules, as they taught you the difference between right and wrong, and gave guidance and provided instruction each time you learned something new about life. As you received training in your early childhood years through adolescence, it was a time of preparation for the next phase of your life. The more training you received, the more prepared you'd be to handle the next season of your life.

Time to play the game. It is much like the training the football team gets from their coach before the next season begins. The team goes through rigorous, boot-camp-like activity for more than three or four months preparing for opening day.

Bully Me...Oh NO!!!

What if one of the key players of the football team decided to quit just minutes before the first game of the season, because he felt he couldn't take it anymore? It's not acceptable, because it's time to play the game.

You are in that season of life, where it's almost time to play the game. This is not the time to quit or give up. This is the time to exercise all that you been taught and use what you've learned to stand up to your opponent, and play the game. This is the time for you to embrace life and share your ideas, gifts and talents with the world. You have been in training and making preparation all these years. Now it's your time to shine. And no one can take your place.

The bully may have come from a home where there was no one to nurture or provide love. Perhaps the bully's basic needs haven't always been met. But when the bully shows up, it's time to play the game of life, and use what you've been taught. The bully is your test to take what you've learned at home and put it into action. Remember you have something the bully needs and wants—"**Love.**"

You are a winner! In this case, the bully is the obstacle or hurdle you must get over. So, for you to disappear from the scene forever, would mean you are a loser. And that, you are not. You've had too much training and prepping, and your parents have invested too much time and money for you to quit now. You cannot give up, or give in, because you, my friend, are a winner! Now, back to the game.

You have many options. You can choose to stand up for yourself, ignore the bully until you can get help, laugh (be a good sport), walk away, even question their motive, etc. Whatever your reaction, the bully's action against you should be reported right away.

Build your team. Everyone needs to have a support team (parents, counselor, youth pastor). In *Bully Me? . . .NO MORE!!!*, a sample is given, for you need to know that you are not alone. Your support team is there to provide the help that you need.

These are the people that you trust, that believe in you and have your best interest at heart. They are the ones who can speak an encouraging word, build you up when needed and get you through the adversity when it comes your way. They should take action immediately, and should remain consistent with follow-up until the bullying stops.

Green Light. Teenager, it's springtime in your life. It's time for you to put into practice what you've learned in training, have respect for yourself and others, and show some brotherly love. Permission granted to step into the spring of life and live.

Honor life, and choose to be the winner that you already are.

"*The thief cometh not, but for to steal, and to kill, and to destroy: I have come that you might have life, and life more abundantly*" (John 10:10).

Action Item: Watch the Wizard of Oz DVD. Find the two characters in the movie that are obvious bullies. You will see that both are cowards. What a wonderful example of a bully. ☺

This movie will help you understand that the bully is merely a distraction to keep you from focusing on the more important things in life like school, your future, your goals-long and short term. Now let's focus on your amazing life.

Honoring the Life You Were Given

Have you ever asked yourself, "Why am I here?" or "What was I created for?" Have you ever wondered why you are here today, and at this particular time in history?

God planned it that way. He had a specific purpose for you to be born at this time, and He has something special for you to do while you are here. So you need to find out what your assignment is. That's right; you are here on assignment from Almighty God.

In fact, before you were born, you were in His thoughts. You are very important to God. You are so important that He even knows how many hairs you have on your head. Yes, He loves you that much, and there is something here on earth that only you can do.

Your life is incomplete until you have done what you are called to do. It may take a little time to prepare for your assignment. It may mean sharpening your skills, rehearsing or taking lessons. It may require studying intensely or doing extensive research. So plan on being here for awhile, and while you're here, make your journey a pleasant experience. Now get ready to enjoy the ride of life.

Bully Me. . .Oh NO!!!

As you realize your purpose, you will become a better manager of your gifts and talents, and things in your life will seem to come together supernaturally. This is where you'll be able to experience the peace of God and walk in the fullness of His joy.

Yes, you are here on assignment.

Don't stop searching until you find out what you were called to do to honor Him.

"Love" Notes

"Love" notes are merely a reflection of a parents' love. Do you remember receiving that **"love"** note from Mom that you found tucked away in your coat pocket, or the one in your boxed lunch? There was something about that nod of approval, or pat on the back from your Dad when you were younger? Just one **"love"** note, or nod of approval, carried you for a long time.

This is what they were saying to you, as they continued to wish you well, and in those silent moments as they held their breath in observance of you:

"I Love You"

II.

A Mirror Image
Looking back at you

What's the Matter with You?

Not feelin' the love? Give yourself a hug. Feels like everybody's messin' with you? Well, sometimes you just have to encourage yourself. Be determined to think happy thoughts. Learn to be grateful for the little things; be thankful for a bed to sleep in, and the comfort of a home. You could be homeless.

If you woke up with a chip on your shoulder, you have to knock it off before you leave the house. It's one thing to wake up grumpy because you didn't sleep well, or went to bed too late the night before; but, everyday is not acceptable. Every day can't be a bad day. So, if you wake up in a bad mood every day, then you need to do something about it.

You can wake up happy every day, if you choose to. However, you must decide to take charge of your thoughts and emotions. While you're doing that, show your parents some love today – a kind word, a hug, a note of thanks. And know that you're going to be just fine, because life is about to get better for you.

As you read on you will find some practical solutions to many of your concerns. Now all you will need is a little faith and an open heart to receive them. Keep reading. :)

"Love" Note

"Hey Son (Daughter),

*I've been waiting to hear from you,
Because whatever's bothering you
Affects me too.*

*Can we talk it over?
Just me and you?*

*I love you more than you'll ever know."
(Dad) (Mom)*

"Love" Notes are merely a reflection of a parents' love.

Bully Me...Oh NO!!!

Looking in the Mirror

How confident are you? If you're like most teens you could use a little help in this area. In the following list of questions, there's no perfect or one right answer. Take a moment to respond to the questions below to measure your level of confidence.

Which word or phrase best describes the way you feel most of the time? You may use these words to fill in the blanks or complete these on a separate sheet of paper. *{Happy, joyful, peaceful, comfortable, content, great, "so, so," angry, alone, afraid, fearful, in pain, lonely, mad, sad, unhappy, or worried}*

1. Use the words in the {} to fill in the blanks, or you can use other words to describe how you feel.

    a. I am _____ most of the time.
    b. I am usually _____ when I'm with my friends.
    c. I am always _____ when I go to school.
    d. I feel _____ in the presence of others.
    e. When I am _____, I prefer to be alone.

2. How does it make you feel when someone treats you in an unkind manner? Circle one:

Bully Me. . .Oh NO!!!

    a. Doesn't bother me
    b. I don't care
    c. Not good
    d. It hurts.

3. How do you respond when someone seeks to harm you?   Circle one:
    a. Ignore them, and walk away
    b. Laugh
    c. Report it immediately
    d. Cry
    e. Do nothing

The questions you have answered can help you assess where you are emotionally. The answers you have provided can also be useful if you choose to receive counseling later.

You have Options: Now, you be the judge. Could you use a little more confidence? Are you in the presence of positive people most of the time, or not at all? It helps to surround yourself with positive people, and to think on good things, on things that are praiseworthy; to be grateful and give thanks. As you concentrate or focus on the more positive things in life, you'll feel better about yourself.

Teenager: "Getting to Know You"
(Searching for the best "U")

In the first 8 years of your life, you developed the basic skills necessary for living. The various skill sets learned in adolescence, if properly guided have exposed many of your God-given gifts or talents.

Now that you've become a teenager, this is perhaps the best time to do self-examination. So let's begin by asking a few important questions.

How well do you know yourself? Exactly who are you? And what do you want out of life? What makes you happy? What makes you feel sad? What are your favorite things? . . .your favorite foods? Do you have a hobby? What do you like to do?

What do you want to accomplish in life? Have you set any goals? Do you have a one year plan? How about a five year plan? What do you see yourself doing in the next ten years? How will you make a positive difference in the world?

Who are your friends? Do you influence them? Or do they influence you? Do you lead or follow? Are you a good friend? Do you share good information or are you a hoarder? Do you care about the welfare of others or think only of yourself?

Bully Me. . .Oh NO!!!

What can you do to improve your life? Or make a positive difference in the lives of those around you? What do you need help doing? Do you know how to get the assistance you need? Don't be afraid to ask.

It's important that you get to know yourself, so that you can love the person that you are, and value all that God has created "you" to be. Equally important is your understanding the specific purpose for which you were created. You need to know that you are not here by accident.

There's no better time than your teen years to discover your purpose in life, or to at least begin to ask yourself some important questions about why you are here. You can begin by answering these same questions in the workbook.

"For I know the thoughts that I think toward you, saith the Lord, thoughts of peace, and not of evil, to give you an expected end {to give you a future and a hope}" (Jeremiah 29:11).

Eliminating "Bullymotions"?

Are you suffering from "**bullymotions**" - the negative effects of being the 'bully victim?' If you've been negatively affected because you were bullied or are fearful that it may happen to you, you have "**bullymotions**."

When you feel angry, worried, or afraid, you need to address those feelings. Here's something else you need to know. You do have options.

If you choose (notice, I said choose, because it is a choice that you're making) to get upset about something that happened, it's best to release it right away—forgive that person and let it go—to maintain a peaceful state of mind. If you choose not to let it go, anger or bitterness may surface.

If it's anger that you have, you must first acknowledge that you are angry, then identify the root cause of that anger. Anger is a feeling that stems from your reaction to something that happened to you, or regarding something you care about, that you didn't like. Ask yourself, if it is something that just happened, or have you been carrying it around for awhile?

Once you have determined the reason for your anger, you will need to forgive the person for their actions which led to your anger. Anyone who broods over a negative incident for an extended period of time, rather than forgive, will eventually move from a state of being angry to bitterness.

While anger stems from something that happened to you that you didn't like or agree with, bitterness is an extension of that anger. Bitterness is much stronger than being angry and is more deeply rooted, because you have given the matter concentrated thought over time.

In other words, it's seasoned with time. And being bitter can adversely affect your health over time. Try to forgive. It makes the healing process easier.

Eliminating "Bullymotions"

So what are you going to do if someone has angered you or caused you pain? Suggestion: Forgive them - instantly. Forgiveness and healing go hand-in-hand. As you forgive, healing will come.

Option: If you've found that you're in a happy state of mind, stay there, by thinking happy thoughts and keeping a positive attitude throughout the day. Continue to build and work on your dreams and aspirations, as you think of how you can help to make the world a better place.

"Forgive and you will be forgiven" (Luke 6:37b).NKJV

Taking Action

Other Options: If you are upset, choose to forgive, and do it immediately. If you are fearful or afraid tell someone what you are feeling and why you feel that way.

If the person you tell does not assist you, or get help for you, keep talking to the people that you trust until you get the support you need. It's that important, and someone needs to understand that your life could be in danger. While you're talking, pray, until you receive the help you need.

Are you hurting from something that was said about you, or do you feel alone because groups of your peers have formed that don't include you? You must make it a point to find other friends-people that you have something in common with, and that value you as a person.

Is your pain physical? Physical pain is a warning sign that something is not right in your body. Has someone inflicted pain on you with force through a physical action? An adult needs to address this action against you. Don't try to handle it yourself. Speak up. Tell someone that you trust.

And if you are unhappy, or worried, talk, talk, talk; and keep talking to that responsible adult, or person that you trust. Be open to receive professional counseling and open for conversation with your parents, as these feelings may need to be monitored professionally for you.

If you are in a place where you are alone, or feel lonely, always know that God is there with you and available for you. He has placed angels around you for your protection.

He is listening for your voice and offers comfort. He will be your safety net if you acknowledge Him. There is no better friend than He. *"He is a friend that sticketh closer than a brother"* (Proverbs 18:24), and He will be with you to the end.

If you need to be encouraged, you can't wait for someone to come along and pick you up emotionally. Sometimes you have to encourage yourself; and say it in an audible voice so you can hear it.

Taking Action: For example: If you need to be strengthened in the area of self-esteem, you can say, "I am confident." "I am enthusiastic and excited about life."

You can also say, "I am excited about tomorrow. I'm sure everything's going to be alright." "This is going to be a great day." And if things haven't worked out well for you, say, "I am thankful to have another chance to try it again." "I'm moving forward." "Tomorrow will be a better day." ☺

Bully Me...Oh NO!!!

III.

Living with Great Expectation
for a great life

Practice living each day with great expectation for a great life. Plan to succeed in all that you do.

Bully Me. . .Oh NO!!!

Why? . . . Why Not?
Watch what you're sayin'

Sometimes you receive the outcome you're expecting and sometimes you don't. There are various reasons why. The idea is to figure out the why's or why not's, if you can, and move on.

Maybe the time is not right, or perhaps the desired outcome would have brought you harm in some way. Don't linger in the disappointment of it, for to linger is time wasted that you cannot get back.

In this section, we will discuss one of the reasons why we don't receive what we desire to happen for or to us. Have you ever asked, "Why did this happen to me?" or "How did that happen?" Everything we go through in life has an outcome. But did you know that your "attitude" affects your end result?

Your words can also affect your outcome as well. If you are constantly saying what you don't want to happen, it probably will happen, because you are spending more time on what you don't want. Focus on what you want to happen and plan for it to take place. This is called faith, believing in what you are hoping for. These two action words, faith and belief, work together well.

Without word control, you might only receive what is expected, and not necessarily your heart's desire. The expected outcome is the norm, or the average, and is usually accomplished by applying minimal effort or, as some would say, 'doing next to nothing.' We could say then, that the expected outcome is usually what you allow (to happen). There's something else you need to know.

You have to have a little faith. The Bible says that *"faith without works is dead"* (James 2:26).

Here's the challenge: Build your faith muscle with encouraging words. Now work your faith muscle. I challenge you to bring your faith to life; and to work your faith. ☺

"I Expected That"

For every challenge, for every test, there is an expected outcome, and there is an actual outcome; but the actual outcome is determined by "our attitude." Whether it's intellectually stimulating or physically challenging, you must prepare, study, exercise, condition yourself, or your mind, to accomplish it (get it done).

If you have done these things, you will naturally meet or exceed your expectation. In most instances, your motivation and enthusiasm kick in and you automatically exceed (your) expectation because of that momentum.

Always strive to be better than what the average person expects of you. The average person does not expect you to do well, nor for you to be your best at all times. Therefore, they expect the worse, or at least less than good.

I'm sure you've heard the phrase, "It is as good as can be expected." What does that phrase mean? It is the bare minimum, or at the very least, the "status quo," and is achieved with little effort, inferring very little hope.

Call it human nature if you will, but it actually takes effort to stay positive. Make an effort to say positive affirmations, speak positively to others, think positive thoughts, and do kind deeds every day.

Decide to live above the "status quo" by changing the way you think. Set your mind on higher heights, to do greater things, to rise above expectation. Never let anyone have the pleasure of saying "I expected that," because things didn't go well for you.

Always offer the element of surprise every time, because you are so good at what you do. Live above and beyond their expectation. And simply do it for your pleasure, not for theirs.

Great Expectation

Refuse to be ordinary and live just to get by, or barely make it from day to day. Plan to succeed in all that you do and honor Him in all that you do.

Strive only to be your best, and to receive only the best that life can offer, for you deserve to have a great life. Remember, you are one of God's creations. You are His gift of life, and His plan for you is only good. So live your life with great expectation!

"...I came that they may have and enjoy life, and have it in abundance (to the full, till it overflows)" (John 10:10 amp)

IV.
Power Play

Respecting Authority, Self and Others

"Love" Note

*"Wish we could tell you how much we love you.
If you only knew how much we care,
You wouldn't storm away angry
Or walk away with your nose in the air."*

*We still love you,
Mom & Dad*

When was the last time your sent your parents a message of **"love?"** ☺ You can do it now.

"I'm A Teenager . . . What do you expect?"

How many times have you heard an adult say: "They're teenagers, what do you expect?" For some reason, society gives teens the green light to rebel (resist) authority. There are no excuses for unacceptable behavior at any age.

Now, for many of you, rebellion is not an issue. However, you could be instrumental in helping one of your peers get through this phase of life. So please keep reading.

It makes no difference if you are a toddler or teen, you have to respect rules and obey authority. Accepting less than a person's best is a welcome mat for failure at any age. A rebellious teen can easily become a bully.

Let's say it again. Just because you are a teenager does not give you the right to rebel against authority. An endorsement of this type could lead to criminal activity later. And rebellion is the root cause of most problem-prone teens.

Let's define "rebellious" and its' root word, "rebel," so you can understand why it is not acceptable. These are my definitions by the way.

"Rebellious"- the activity of doing wrong intentionally, or going against the expected right way; intentional wrong behavior, or unacceptable behavior done on purpose.

A "rebel" is one who goes against the path of the accepted norm, the right way, or against the path of justice; one who does wrong intentionally by refusing to abide by the rules. Teenager, as you become more outspoken and begin to be recognized for your opinion, beliefs and ideas, you will begin to brand yourself by your behavior (actions) and the words that you speak. This is another reason why it is not o.k. to "rebel" against the parental authority in your home.

If you respect and obey your parental authority, you'll stay clear of unseen danger and avoid trouble. Just as you are expected to honor the rules at home, there are laws and ordinances in the real world that you must obey, or be punished.

Home is where you practice obedience, good manners and social etiquette, which can serve as a gateway to your becoming an outstanding citizen. Good citizenship will yield to your leaving an indelible impression on the world, establishing a legacy, and making a contribution to society. As discussed earlier, you are in this world for a reason.

"To whom much is given, much shall be required."
(taken from Luke 12:48)

"Honor"
Respecting the authority you're under

Did you know that you can add years onto your life by honoring your parents? Honoring your parents brings honor to your life. You are commissioned to honor, respect and obey your parents, for it's the right thing to do. There are few exceptions where the legal system must intervene, but that is not for the majority of the individuals reading this book.

Let's take a closer look at what it means to give honor to someone. According to Merriam Webster Dictionary, to honor is "to regard or treat with admiration and respect." For the purpose of this book, I'd like to add to that definition of honor, as "a respectful recognition of one's place of authority, position, or office."

Since the day you were born, your parents have taken the responsibility to protect and provide a safe living environment for you to dwell in. They have fed, clothed, and provided for your basic needs. Do you remember the all-niters when you weren't feeling well and couldn't sleep? Who stayed with you until you went back to sleep? ;)

Have you ever taken a moment to think about the sacrifices made and time spent getting you from point A to B for all of your extracurricular activities like boy scouts, girl scouts, band practice, choir rehearsal, plays, special projects, not to mention the rides to school, etc; or the extra little things to make you happy when they needed to do something else?

All of their sacrifices were made to help you become the great individual that you are destined to become. And there's so much more.

Recognize today that the least you can do is to honor your parents with your words when you speak to them, honor them with your love, in your actions, and in every kind thought you can think of concerning them.

You can live long and finish strong, if you honor your parents. So honor them, because it's the right thing to do.

Something to think about: Consider yourself a guest in your parents' home, and realize that guests are not required to stay. Don't wear out your welcome. :)

"Honor your father and your mother, so that you may live long in the land the LORD your God is giving you" (Exodus 20:12) niv.

If They Had Only Listened

Too often children, teenagers and young adults do things they later regret. Sometimes we hear them say "If I had only listened;" referring to those times when Momma said, "It is better to obey," or Dad said, "No, you can't go." But, because of their disobedience, they have suffered the consequence of that one wrong decision.

Unfortunately, you can't undo what you've done in the past, but you can move forward. It's less painful, however, to learn from the mistakes of others, than to experience the trouble for yourself. That's why parents are called responsible adults.

They have been given authority over you and are responsible for your welfare. The authority they have is ordained by God. The responsible adult in your life wants you to be well-adjusted in every area of your life. This is something that doesn't just happen. It's something that you have to work at continuously, and walking in obedience to authority plays a major role in it.

This topic prompted the following survey of willing adults. :) The question was: If you could do it over, would you choose to obey your parents, based on the one bad experience you had when you chose not to obey? Here are the results.

Bully Me. . .Oh NO!!!

Out of 100 adults surveyed 50 said yes; 3 said, "I always obeyed." Only 3 said "no." Still waiting for the other 44 responses to come in (email, FB). :(

TALK:

One Conversation Could Make a Difference

"Love" Note

To my teenage son and daughter,

"Your concerns are important to me.
What bothers you also bothers me.
Let' talk it over.
Let's think things through.

Together we can make it.
If we talk it over,
Just me and you."

Love you,
Mom & Dad

Action Item: Your parents need to know that you are doing o.k., because they are responsible for your well-being. And they really do care. Talk to them every day. Love them in your own special way. Do something nice for them, just because.

Bully Me...Oh NO!!!

Respecting Self:

A Teen's Decision

Every action you take in life begins with a decision. Whether you decide to lead or follow the crowd, to do the right thing or do wrong, it's a decision you must make.

How much thought do you give to the decisions you make on a daily basis? At this crucial stage in your life, it's o.k. to think things through twice. In fact, from now on, take as long as you need to think before you take any action.

In this section of the book, we'll look at a few examples. Let's start with your friends. Always use caution when selecting your circle of friends, or associates, for these are the people who will have great influence over the decisions you are making. They will affect your life either directly, or indirectly, depending on the situation.

When something becomes a fad, or simply the thing to do, among teen peer groups, there is a tendency to follow the crowd. It's called "peer-pressure," and because most teens want to be like their peers, they just do it.

Let's take the following illustration for example. Tattoos are very popular, and getting one is the popular thing to do. A lot of teens are getting them. But, one important question you might ask is: "What is a tattoo?" (A tattoo is a permanent mark or design made on the body by insertion of pigment through ruptures in/under the skin.) You might also ask, "Will it add value to me?"

Here's something to think about before you take action. You may want to:

1. Research the pros and cons of getting one.
2. Research the process and cost(s) involved.
3. Find out if it can be removed, how long it takes, and how much it cost to remove it.
4. Check with your medical doctor first, especially if you have health concerns.

What does this have to do with bullying? Here's the parallel between the two. The negative effects of the bully's actions against you can leave a permanent scar on the inside, if you don't speak up right away. The more prolonged your feelings of hopelessness, fear or despair, the more permanent or serious the damage can become.

Action Item: It's important to release the hurt by forgiving, and to let someone know right away. Three things take place when you do this. 1. You allow the possibility of hope to take root in your life again, and 2. You don't internalize it, or keep rehearsing it, and 3. You are not forced to work it out alone. Taking this kind of immediate action will keep your mind, spirit and emotions calm and lead to better health and safety overall.

Teenager, Teenager What Will It Be?

While you are making some of the most important decisions in this phase of your life, it's during this time that you may feel added pressure to conform. It's called "peer pressure." And you must choose, when you're in the presence of your friends or peers, whether to go with the flow, or go with what you know is right (the right thing to do).

Your peers are those who you like, or admire, respect, want to be like, look up to, hang around and observe up close, or from a distance. They are your age, may have similar interests or dislikes, and can be influential or controversial.

A Matter of Choice. Pressure is applied when your moral standard or value system is in conflict with what your peers may be doing. And your decision to, or not to go along with what they are doing causes a division, rift or separation between you and that person or the crowd.

It's important for you to understand the power of your decision-making skills; for the decisions you make today will affect you for the rest of your life.

When you reach the age of accountability - able to discern right from wrong - you are responsible for the choices you make. And every decision made is a step toward your future.

Bully Me...Oh NO!!!

The choices you make can determine a life of success and peace, or lead to a life of disappointments and regrets. You choose to be happy or sad, to have joy, to be content, to show compassion, or disdain, to go right or go left, to be a leader, or one who follows the crowd.

That is why you must be strong, take a stand, be confident in who you are, do the right thing, and not buckle under pressure.

This is where self-esteem – having the confidence to take a stand for what you believe is right, and doing the right thing, is important; even if it means standing alone because of that one right decision. Self-esteem plays a major role in you making good decisions on a daily basis, and is a derivative (reflective) of behaviors that were reinforced at home.

Some critical questions to ask yourself before making a major decision:

1. Will this decision bring harm or be an inconvenience to me or someone else?
2. Will this decision yield continuous positive results?
3. Is it necessary?
4. Is it cost-effective? Does it fit within the proposed budget?
5. How will this action affect my future?

....*be strong in the Lord, and in the power of His might.* (Ephesians 6:10b)

Cyber Space? "Can You Handle It?"
The power is in your hands.

Do you respect your neighbors in cyberspace? Do you think about your message before you release it to the world? Or are you a cyber bully - one who sends negative or degrading messages through social mediums?

This may sound like a silly question, but if you send one derogatory message on any one of the social media platforms, you could be labeled a cyber bully, because the damage is harmful, humiliating, and cannot be retrieved.

How are you handling your space (on the web)?

You can be quoted in cyberspace for decades because of the great network of social mediums on the world-wide-web. The written comments or statements made on social medium platforms become your spoken word.

It can be very damaging if you are speaking in an unkind manner. Notice, here we are using the word "spoken." This is because in social media your communication speaks volumes to everyone who reads or sees it.

Ever hear of the phrase? "Think before you leap!" If you know you can't swim, why would you jump into deep waters? And if you know you can't tread

Bully Me...Oh NO!!!

water, why would you launch out into the deep? It's a no brainer. You either "sink or swim."

The same applies to cyberspace. Don't dish out, something you can't take. If you want others to speak kindly of you, speak kindly of them.

It is similar to the golden rule: "Do unto others as you would have them do unto you." It's a great way to live, and a great rule to practice for the rest of your life, if you desire to live peaceably with all mankind.

Ask yourself, before you send that email message, face book, tweet, or link someone in: "Will this message edify, or encourage this person in some way?" If the answer is "yes," then send it. If the answer is "no," then don't send it.

So, here are a few cyber rules to remember:
1. Treat your friend(s) in cyberspace like they are your kindest neighbor or your dearest friend.
2. Before you send a message, ask yourself: "Is it all good?" If the answer is "no," don't send it.
3. Think twice before you post or send a message.

Option: If you become a cyber bully victim, responding to the sender with a message like this can help you begin to heal from its' negative effects:

"The steps I take today are directly linked to my future. That is why I must remain focused on achieving my goals in life. Therefore, I selectively choose to forgive you for the actions you've taken against me." (Your name)

V.
A Work In Progress
Every day is another step into your future

You Can . . .

You can do all things, for you are God's handiwork, a wonderful creation, His masterpiece. One of the keys to building your level of confidence is accepting who you are, and learning to speak affirmatively when referring to yourself.

To speak affirmatively you would say "I can. . ." instead of "I can't." And if you practice saying phrases that begin with "I will. . .," "I expect to. . ." and "I plan to . . .," it will become more natural in time.

"Your words" – the words that you say - are so very powerful, that it might be always be in your best interest to do your homework before engaging in meaningful conversation. It is wise to get an understanding of your subject matter, to think it over, and then speak.

The more positive your speech, the more positive your actions will be also. And as you learn to think of others in a more positive way, you will find it easier to do or perform random acts of kindness.

Your thoughts become your spoken words, for you will say what you constantly think about. And your actions will follow your words. So until your thoughts are totally positive, be selective with your word choices.

As you turn the negative words, or statements that you make into positive statements and affirmations, so too, will your life begin to reflect the words that you are speaking over yourself. The goal is to speak positive words at all times. They will change the course of your day. Be confident in who you are and who you are becoming. Be somebody who makes a difference in the world. Be determined to do something great. The world is waiting on your ideas, discoveries, and dreams to manifest.

I know you can . . . DO IT!

As you place your hand in God's hand, He will help to manifest all of these things in your life as you speak/say them each day. He will continue to renew your mind and spirit as you spend time with Him. He just needs to hear from you, and for you to invite Him to be your friend. There's more good news. . .

"I will praise thee; for I am fearfully and wonderfully made: marvelous are thy works;..." (Psalm 139:14)

Say What You Want
Act on It, and Become What You Speak

If you encountered even one bully in your lifetime, you probably needed encouragement afterward. Know that it really doesn't matter what others think about you. Their opinion is not important. And as you move forward, remember to say only those things that you desire to become, then, have the faith to believe it will be so.

You can actually change your life with the words you speak over yourself. On the next few pages you will find more than 200 words for you to use to re-shape your world.

The words provided are to increase your inner strength, and to serve as confidence builders. You must remember never to think too highly of yourself or allow your ego to become inflated. To do so would be considered egotistical.

But on the same note, one needs to be confident in who he is, in order to handle the issues of life. Therefore, the goal is to have a balance of positive self-esteem and assertive confidence. And that takes some practice.

Add this list of 200+ adjectives/word phrases to your personal vocabulary for that purpose. And let's begin rebuilding your inner spirit to change the course of your life today.

Bully Me...Oh NO!!!

200+ Words of Encouragement

These life-changing words are provided to help you turn negative thoughts and words into positive ones.

Adaptable, admirable, adorable, adventurous, affable, affectionate, agreeable, alert, amicable, ambitious, astonishing, astoundingly charming, athletic, attractive, authentic, awesome, beautiful (inwardly and outwardly), bold, brave, bright(my future is), brilliant, calm, caring, charming, cheerful, chosen, classy, comforting, commendable (my work was), compassionate, confident, conscientious, considerate, cooperative, courteous, courageous, creative, credible, dashing, dazzling personality, debonair, decisive, delightful, desire to live long and finish strong, determined to make a positive difference in the world, determined to succeed, destined for greatness, diligent, diplomatic, disciplined, distinguished, dynamic personality, easy to get along with, eager, effervescent, efficient, elated, elegant, electrifying, eloquent, eminent, enchanting, encouraging, energetic, entertaining in a good way, enthusiastic, essential, excellent character, excited about life, exemplary, exhilarating, extremely positive, exuberant, fabulous, faithful, fair, fair-minded, a fantastic friend, fascinating, fearless, focused, forgiven, forgiving, friendly, fun, hilariously funny, generous, gentle, genuine, genius (have the nature of a), good, good-natured, a gracious lady, a great example, hard-working, happy, harmonious, helpful, hilarious, honest, honorable, humorous, impartial, impressive, an independent thinker, indispensable, industrious, inquisitive, instinctive,

Bully Me...Oh NO!!!

intellectual, intelligent, interesting, intuitive, inventive, irreplaceable, jolly, full of joy, joyous, joyful, jovial, keenly alert, a key element, kind, kind-hearted, a kingdom builder for Christ, knowledgeable, laudable, a leader, level-headed (level), a light in darkness, likeable, lively, lovely, loving, loyal, magnificent, marvelous, melodic personality, mighty man of valor, modest, more than a conqueror, neat, needed, nice, noble, obedient, optimistic, outstanding, patient, at peace, peaceful, personable, a pioneer, placid, pleasant, polite, a positive force, positively good, powerful, practical, precious, proactive, productive, punctual, quick, quiet, a rare gem, receptive to all that is good, for real, refined, reflective, reliable, remarkable, reserved, resilient, resolute, resourceful, responsible, reverent, romantic, sassy, secure, sedate, seemly, selective, self-assured, sensational, sensible, sensitive to others needs, sincere, skillful, smart, sociable, have a splendid personality, steadfast, strong, stunning, successful, superb, sweet, sympathetic, talented, tenacious, thoughtful, tidy, tranquil, trustworthy, truthful, unbiased, understanding, unique, unshakable, unstoppable, have unusual gifts, upbeat, valiant, valuable, versatile, a victor, victorious, vigilant, virtue, virtuous, a visionary, vivacious, a cheerful volunteer, warmhearted, willing to forgive, a winner, full of wisdom, wise, witty, wonderful, a person of my word, young, youthful . . . Isn't this exciting? You can add as many words to the list as you like.

Options: You can activate the power of the spoken Word (what God says about you) in your life too. To do this, turn to page 107.

Now choose five or more words that you see in yourself, or have a desire to become.

For example a young man might say: "I am a mighty man of valor. I am confident and bold. I am intelligent. I have the nature of a genius."

A young lady might say: "I am pleasant and polite. I will use my impartial judgment to love the unlovable, and forgive, and I will continue to be graceful in the affairs of life."

Always:
1. Use confidence when you speak.
2. Speak these words daily to encourage yourself.
3. Say them several times a day.

Then:
4. Go a step further and use these words in a positive and affirming way to encourage others.
5. This is another way to defeat the bully. Yes. You can even say something positive about the bully. Notice his reaction.

Action Item: A glossary has been provided for the preferred definition of key words provided. These words are to help the bully victim go through the healing process and to help re-build a broken spirit. See page 110-111.

Bully Me...Oh NO!!!

Change the direction of your life by saying only good things daily. One of the greatest things you can do is to say what the Word of God says about you; and it is always good.

For example, you may have heard the phrase, "I can do anything I put my mind too." But God's Word says: *"I can do all things through Christ who strengthens me"* (Philippians 4:13). So, you can speak this powerful Word over yourself by saying, "I can do all things through Christ who strengthens me."

If you are discouraged, His Word says, ". . .Be strong and of a good courage; be not afraid, . . .for the Lord thy God is with thee whithersoever thou goest" (Joshua 1:9). You can say, "I won't be afraid for God is with me wherever I go. I will stay encouraged no matter what it looks like."

If you feel hopeless, and nothing seems to be going right for you, His Word says, "Nay, in all these things we are more than conquerors through Him that loved us" (Romans 8:37). You can say, "God loves me, and I am more than a conqueror."

If you feel weak, His Word says, "God is our refuge and strength, a very present help in trouble" (Psalm 46:1); and "Let the weak say I am strong" (Joel 3:10b). And you can say, "I am strong, for God is my refuge and strength."

Bully Me...Oh NO!!!

If you are fearful, "Fear thou not; for I am with thee: be not dismayed; for I am thy God: I will strengthen thee; yea, I will help thee; yea, I will uphold thee with the right hand of my righteousness" (Isaiah 41:10). And say, "**God upholds me with His righteous right hand, therefore I will not fear, and I will not be afraid.**"

You don't have to be afraid for His Word says, "The Lord is on my side; I will not fear: what can man do unto me?" (Psalm 118:6); and "For God hath not given us the spirit of fear; but of power, and of love, and of a sound mind" (2 Timothy 1:7). You can simply repeat these awesome verses and say, "**The Lord is on my side; I will not fear: what can man do unto me?**" and "**God has not given me the spirit of fear, but a spirit of power, a spirit of love, and of a sound mind.**"

If you are disturbed about bullies, life issues, or seemingly impossible situations, Let God keep you in perfect peace according to Isaiah 26:3. And say, "**Because I keep my mind stayed on Him, I have (will have) perfect peace.**"

After you've decreed God's Word over your life, stand tall. Believe, and keep standing, for the Word(s) you've just spoken will continue to bring positive changes in your life.

Bully Me...Oh NO!!!

Make A Contribution

You can stay out of trouble if you
Just avoid strife.
Manage your thoughts and
Live a peaceful life.

You can decide to make a contribution
And prove the stats wrong.
Be better than average,
But you must remain strong.

You can do more than make it
You can go way beyond that
Yes, you can be an example for others to live by,
Set goals and stay on track.

It's time for you to make a contribution.
Start today. Don't look back.

I know you can . . . "Just Do It!!"

"Just do it!" A phrase made popular by Nike

VI.

Bully Tips

(using preventive measures)

Bully Me...Oh NO!!!

(Spoken in) **"Love"**

"Hey Son, what's the matter?
Are you o.k.?
We haven't heard a word from you all day.

Your mom and I are concerned about you.
You are always in our thoughts.
You have a minute, Son? **- Let's talk.**"

Dad

Symptoms of a Bully Victim

If you are experiencing the following symptoms, it may be an indication that you have been bullied.

- A sudden change in eating habits – very little appetite, not eating at all, etc.
- Sudden noticeable change in personality, i.e., a change from passive to aggressive
- Feelings of helplessness or decreased self-esteem
- Feeling sick or having frequent headaches suddenly
- Loss of interest in school, social or work-related activities
- An inability to communicate or express oneself clearly
- A decline in academic grades
- A change in sleeping habits, insomnia
- Becomes withdrawn, or extremely introverted

Bully Me. . .Oh NO!!!

If You Are Being Bullied
Here's what you can do

1. Don't panic! Do take immediate action!

2. Talk to a responsible adult, including your parent(s), school official, family member/friend that has your best interest at heart, without compromise. This is your support system.

3. If it's physical, it's not wise to fight back. (This could be gang-related activity.) Go get help.

4. One occurrence is too many. If it continues consider professional counseling.

5. Make it a point to stay busy or involved in extra-curricular activities that you enjoy.

6. Change your routes to school or work.

7. Try not to be alone in remote places. Walk with friends in multiples.

8. Be supportive of others too. It helps to think of and be kind to others.

9. Stay encouraged, even if you have to encourage yourself. Think positive thoughts.

10. It is important that you release the sting of the attack and forgive the bully right away. And remember, you have done nothing wrong.

Action Item: If you forgive, healing will come. If you forgive right away, healing will come quickly.

Applying Life Principles

1. Always respect authority (parents included).
2. Begin each day with a positive attitude.
3. Refresh your thoughts often with positive words.
4. Keep a bright smile on the inside, and it will be reflected naturally (in your smile).
5. Show enough kindness to make a difference in someone else's life every day.
6. Pray always for self and others.

7 Tips to Consider Before You Text

Ask yourself:

1. Do I have the right phone number?
2. Is this message worth repeating? (Does it have value?)
3. Is it necessary?
4. Is it uplifting?
5. Is the message timely?
6. Is this message clear? Accurate?
7. Will it shine a positive light on you?

Special Note: Don't text or talk on the phone while driving.

7 Tips to Safeguard You from the Text Bully

1. Weed out your so-called friends.
2. Selectively decide who deserves to have your cell phone number, before you change your phone number.
3. Report any form of threatening or distressing messages (texts/photos/videos) and move on.
4. Treat your cell phone as "private property." Pull out the "No Trespassing" Sign.
5. Avoid contact with the "text bully" to avoid arguments or unnecessary strife.
6. Cut your ties to the messenger once you have made the police report. Have no future communication with them.
7. Try not to take it personally-it could be the wrong number.

Bully Me. . .Oh NO!!!

Healthy Tips for a Healthy Mind

1. Think happy thoughts
2. Be forgiving
3. Keep a smile in your heart.
4. Show kindness to everyone you meet.
5. Encourage others
6. Volunteer to help others
7. Remain calm in tense moments
8. Breathe deeply throughout the day
9. Drink lots of water to keep your body refreshed on the inside
10. Laugh out loud or chuckle quietly, depending on where you are, daily. ☺
11. Eat fresh fruits and vegetables daily.
12. Exercise. Stretch your muscles each day. Go for a walk. Exercise does the body good.
13. Get the rest your body needs each night
14. Pray about everything. Worry about nothing.*

Bonus Health Tip

Get plenty of rest each night. The earlier the better, because the body must be replenished after a full day of school, work, extra-curricular activities, projects etc., that you're involved in.

* A phrase used each morning on the Yolanda Adams Morning Show, Radio One FM.

Bully Tips
Working with the Law
To make the world a better place for us all

1. Know where your local police precinct is and how to get there.
2. Keep, or memorize the phone number of your local police precinct and state police.
3. Always respect law enforcement officers and obey the rules or laws of your local, state and federal government.
4. Make sure you understand the law. If you're not sure, ask. The knowledge you gain could save your life.
5. Be a friend to the law enforcement agencies in your area by getting involved with community projects supported local officers.
6. Look for teen programs within your precinct and take an active role. Go a step further. Be a role model.
7. Be informed. Be safe. Practice safety at all times.

Options: A random act of kindness goes a long way. Once a year, quarterly, or as often as you desire to, do a kind deed for one of your law enforcement officers to show your appreciation.

Bully-Free Pledge

I pledge and promise:
1. To treat others with respect at all times.
2. To tell my parents or responsible adult immediately, if I have been bullied.
3. To tell a responsible adult, if I see someone being bullied.
4. To be a good role model for younger children and not engage in bully activity in any form.
5. To remain alert and cautious in unsupervised areas at school, such as, restrooms, hidden corridors and dark stairwells.
6. To show support to others who have been bullied.

"...for I am a remarkable individual, a gifted student, with a promising future. I am a reflection of the beauty that is bubbling up on the inside of me. And I choose to live my life bully-free."

"You will show me the path that leads to life; for in your presence is fullness of joy..." Ps.16:11

You Made Me Realize

You made me realize how special I was.
There was something I had
 . . . something you wanted
 . . . something you needed
 . . . something you found in me.

There was something in your life
 . . . you were lacking
 . . . you were looking
 . . . you were searching for.
 . . . You just needed
"LOVE."

Bully Me...Oh NO!!!

VII.
LAUGH!!!
...and Laugh Out Loud ☺
It works like medicine

Bully Me...Oh NO!!!

 Learn to laugh, and keep smiling.

Bully Me...Oh NO!!!

If It's Funny, LAUGH!
And "laugh heartily"

You have options:

Sometimes what the bully says hurts a lot, and you may not see any humor in it. You may choose to ignore the bully, shake it off, or walk away, if what is being said makes you feel uncomfortable.

Sometimes what the bully says about you is funny, and sometimes you just have to laugh. While you're laughing, if you can see the humor in it, why not laugh out loud? You'll feel so much better later. Laughter is good for the heart, and 'does the body good.' It works like a medicine, without (the negative) side effects.

Another option for you might be to use lighthearted humor on the bully, then join the crowd with laughter. This is an option, only if you're in a non-threatening environment. The bully will (more than likely) go away defeated.

As a note of caution, always use your better judgment in each scenario. If the bully in your case is an obvious coward, he won't retaliate. Remember, life is as much fun as you make it. So learn to laugh at yourself when no one is around. It's good therapy.

Bully Me...Oh NO!!!

You Have to Admit, It Was Funny

My family always went to church together when I was coming up. At church there was a particular family of six children, who laughed at, or bullied - joker bully type - other children often. Everything was funny to them. Everything!

One particular Sunday evening, when I was in middle school, it was our family's turn to be the brunt of their jokes. Our family consisted of three children; so we were definitely outnumbered. It was not our first time, and it certainly would not be our last.

Well, I must tell you that my dad didn't believe in having a lot of unnecessary bills to pay, so our family usually had an older car. Okay, our car was one of the oldest, if not the oldest car at the church. In fact, my Dad never bought new cars, at least, not after I was born. You probably can guess where I'm going with this one.

So as my dad turned the corner, there they were. The whole family was standing there, along with other church members as one of their teenagers yelled, "Here comes "chitty, chitty, bang-bang," and proceeded to laugh out loud. In fact, the entire family stood there and roared with laughter. You may need to look up "chitty, chitty, bang-bang" to get the picture. I think it's from a movie or something. How did I respond? Well. . .Needless to say, I knew what they were inferring, and how degrading it was supposed to be. But for some reason, I thought it was hilarious, and I started laughing with them, and couldn't stop. In fact, I could not control my laughter, because I had a vision of "chitty, chitty bang-bang" in my head, and I knew our car didn't look anything like that. I, quietly and reverently, chuckled through most of the service, as this stayed on my mind, and I am still laughing today. Why? Because what they said was funny, and it is what it is. **:)**

You Have to Laugh Sometimes

The person that is able to smile at his shortcomings, mishaps, mistakes, or faults usually has a wonderful disposition. Being able to laugh at yourself makes you so much more fun to be around. To the super sensitive person, I encourage you to not let little things get to you. Life is more enjoyable when others can laugh or smile with and about you regarding the little things.

Lighten Up A Little Bit

Sometimes you need to turn off the bad news and listen to some good music, watch a funny movie, or do something pleasant, relaxing and fun. So lighten up! And stop taking life so seriously.

Life is ==➔ ==➔ ==➔moving forward
Learn how to enjoy the ride ☺

The above statement is important because everyone has experienced some form of bullying in their lifetime. It's something you tend not to forget, but we must try not to be too sensitive. Know that it really doesn't matter what they say. Even if what the bully says is true, shake it off. Also, remember that every negative encounter with people in your life is not bullying.

Bully Me. . .Oh NO!!!

Who's the Bully Now?
Watch these reruns (on TV) and find the bully

Here's an activity you can do with your family. The goal is to identify the bully's characteristics as outlined in "Bully Me? . . .NO MORE!!!" and find the bully in each cartoon or sitcom listed below. Sometimes you just need to laugh. So let's laugh! ☺

List of Cartoons:
Bugs Bunny
Popeye
Road Runner
Tweetie Bird

Sitcoms:
Amen
Leave it to Beaver
Room 227
The Jefferson's

Some episodes may have more than one bully. Notice, bullies have similar characteristics; they are selfish, mean-spirited critics desiring attention. They are pitiful, timid, obnoxious, cowardly, sad.

Once you've completed this activity, you'll see the bully in a whole new light. The next time a bully approaches you, think "George Jefferson," or just imagine the "cowardly lion" standing before you. Now that is hilarious. :)

Bully Me...Oh NO!!!

The following movies are suggested for educational purposes and are great for classroom discussion as well. With the exception of the Wizard of Oz, the DVD's are more for learning and less for entertainment as it relates to our subject matter. There are many more examples. You can add your favorites to the list.

DVD's/Movies: (Watch with family and discuss)
The Wizard of Oz (1939)
A Christmas Story (1983)
Back to the Future (1985)
Swimming with the Sharks (1994)

Taking Action. Other things you can do:
There are many creative ways to be proactive against the negative effects of bullying. There are classic children's stories that have obvious bullies in them. Read these classic stories and let your younger siblings, nephews, nieces or cousins identify the bully in each one.

For example, let's take the story of "Little Red Riding Hood," has an obvious bully – the wolf. You might ask them, "Who's the bully here?" Another classic is "Snow White and the Seven Dwarfs." There are many more. Let your young audience identify the bully character in each story. Then discuss why there's no need to fear (be fearful).

Bully Me...Oh NO!!!

Point out the bully character's weak spots and share how important it is to laugh. Make it a positive learning experience. Let them know that laughter is like medicine without the side effects.

I especially like the example given in the "Popeye" cartoons, of how Popeye gains massive strength each time he consumes a can of spinach. Each episode implies that spinach builds his muscles and fortifies his body with exceptional strength. That is what we want to accomplish through these resources, to build your inner spirit with faith-filled, positive words, good thoughts and a great attitude for life.

Confidence Builders
More options

Some sports and structured activities are great confidence builders, especially the sports that you excel in, or those you do well naturally. Sports and muscle moving activities keep you fit physically. When you are physically fit, you just feel better overall.

Walking, and other forms of daily exercise are good, particularly if you're not involved in sports. So keep moving so that your muscles and ligaments don't retire before you do. :)

Here is a list of a few things you might consider. You might have to take lessons, and with lessons you will need to practice. Practice requires discipline, which will lead to excellence. When you are this dedicated to your sport, you have no time for the negative things that used to consume you.

Do you have a hobby or special interest, such as wood shop, CAD drafting, sewing, pattern making, music-vocal/instrumental, to name a few? All sports, including karate, judo, tennis, and more are great disciplines.

Let your talents make room for future scholarships, and more than anything, let them showcase a happier, healthier you.

VIII.

The Stats Don't Lie
It's o.k. to know the stats, but refuse to be one

Bully Me. . .Oh NO!!!

Bully Me. . .Oh NO!!!

Statistics show that:

- We are losing an average of 4,400 young people per year from the effects of bullying.
- Suicide is the 3rd leading cause of death among our youth.
- Half of all suicides among children and teens are related to bullying.
- For every suicide among our youth, there are at least 100 suicide attempts.
- More than 14% of high school students have considered it.
    - 7% of high school students have actually attempted suicide.
- According to Yale University: A bully victim is 2 – 9 times more likely to consider suicide.
    - 10 to 14 yr old girls are at a higher risk.

According to ABC News:

- 30% of all students are either bullies or victims of bullying.
- 160,000 students stay home each day because of the fear of being bullied.

According to the National Institute of Occupational Safety Health (NIOSH)

- Employers are experiencing a loss of employment of up to $19 billion, and a drop in the productivity rate of $3 billion, due to workplace bullying.

Bully Me. . .Oh NO!!!

University of Michigan Case Study

Researchers from the U of M Medical School looked at elementary school students from Ypsilanti, Michigan, who had exhibited conduct problems like bullying. According to Louise O'Brien, Ph.D., Assistant Professor, at University of Michigan's Sleep Disorders Center, "Children who are bullies, or have conduct problems at school, are more likely to be sleepy during the day."

It is possible that poor sleep can lead to bullying or other aggressive behaviors—a major problem that many schools are trying to address today. The researchers found that sleepiness could be caused by many factors, including chaotic home environments, fragmented sleep, or not enough sleep, because of too much electronic stimulus from televisions, cell phones or computers in the bedroom.

This study highlights that good sleep is just as essential to a healthy lifestyle as healthy eating and exercise. O'Brien said the study showed that sleepiness seemed to be the biggest driver of the behavior problems.

Michigan Chronicle, Health, June 8-14, 2011.

Note: How are you sleeping? If you are overly aggressive, your sleeping patterns/conditions may need to be observed.

IX.

"FEAR" NOT!

"For God has not given us the spirit of fear, but of power, and of love, and of a sound mind" (1 Timothy 1:7)

Bully Me...Oh NO!!!

Did you know that "perfect love" casts out fear?

God is love; and His love is perfect love! And in Him, there is no fear.

Bully Me...Oh NO!!!

Addressing the Bully in Your Life
Are you doing your part to turn it around?

Because bullies come in so many forms, it is important to understand who the bully is, so we have provided additional character descriptions below. In no way should you be fearful. Keep reading to find out why.

There's the:

"Brute" – By definition, a brute is a brutal, crude, or insensitive person; like a beast. The brute likes to threaten, kick, hit, trip or push others. Some brutes demand money and may threaten to do harm if that person says "no." This bully might fight you or beat you up, to prove his strength or apparent power over you. **Your options:** Stay far away from the brute. Report it. Don't allow this bully to cause you to fear.

"Classroom Bullies" – are your classmates and usually find a way to cause problems in the classroom. Unfortunately, they are clever enough not to get caught most times. They usually time their attacks or mode of operation in such a way as to point the finger to, or blame the victim that is being bullied. The classroom bully takes pencils, pens, and other personal items he/she thinks will upset you. This bully is more of a pest, a nuisance, and a manipulator and might hit you and blame someone else. **Your options:** You might want to request a seat change. This bully's activities should always be reported, so that your citizenship grade is not affected by his/her behavior.

"Crowd" Bullies – this is usually a group of people (similar to a gang) who work together to make a person feel uncomfortable, invoke fear, threaten or bring physical harm. **Your options:** Always keep authorities informed of gang-like activity. Stay away from crowds. Travel in multiples with people that will be supportive of you after the crowd has disseminated. Talk, and keep talking to your family, school officials, and if necessary the local police authority, if you are being threatened or are in danger of physical harm.

The "Name Caller" – is one who says things that are rude, hurtful or embarrassing, and may insult people because of their race, looks, abilities or religious beliefs. **Your options:** Kill his spirit with kindness. Say something that is nice, but truthful, about this bully. And notice the reaction.

Your "So-Called" Friend – Now this one is more dangerous than all of the others because they appear to be your friend when they are not. This bully can act nice one minute and be mean the next. She might say bad things, tease you or boss you around. The friend bully often makes their victim feel like they deserve to be mistreated, and accuse them of being touchy if they complain about it. It is not unusual for them to gossip or spread ugly rumors, make up stories to get people in trouble, or pressure the other person into doing something they don't want to do.
Your Options: Throughout life you will find that friends come and go for various reasons. It's time to un-friend this friend and let this friend go.

Bully Me. . .Oh NO!!!

The "Joker" – makes his audience laugh by insulting or teasing a person about their size, race, religion, looks, grades, etc., even a person who has medical problems gets no respect from him because this bully loves attention. And when they are done poking fun at their subject, they say it was only a joke. **Your options:** You've got to have a since of humor, because everyone needs a good laugh. So, you can either laugh at yourself, or let him have it. Find something that is hilariously funny, not cruel, to say back to this joker. He will be so outdone. *He who laughs last, laughs best.*

"Kinship" Bully – now this is another tough one because this bully is a family member, and a person that you'll see or be around for the rest of your life. This bully may be an older brother or sister, cousin, aunt, uncle; it may even be your mother or father. Their actions against you may be any form of physical abuse, including hitting, shoving, pushing, fighting; verbal, or non-verbal (a mean look or wincing of the eyes). This bully may have characteristics from any one of the aforementioned bully categories, for they can be a brute, appear to be your friend, pretend like they're just playing, call you names, or gang up on you. The kinship bully is feared most because you feel like you have nowhere to turn for help. **Options:** Is there a grandparent, or other family member that you can trust? Report it to the one adult that can come to your rescue. Keep looking for a way out of the abuse, until you reach a safe, legal place.

Let Hope, Replace Despair

You need to know there is One who is not afraid, and who does not want you to suffer from any form of abuse. And He can conquer any bully anywhere, at anytime. He is God Almighty. *"Vengeance is mine; I will repay saith the Lord"* (Romans 12:19).

That means no matter what, He will take care of your enemies, even if they attack you when no one's around and dare you to tell anyone. What's done in the dark, will be brought to the light. God knows everything and He is not pleased when harm comes to you. In His Word, He promises that He *"will bring to light the hidden things of darkness"* (1 Corinthians 4:5)

So, talk to God about everything, and know that He will make a way of escape for you, even when there seems to be no way. Trust Him and He will bring it to pass. Then look for the open door that He will provide for you to break free of your adversary.

Fear not. Let me say it again. Have no fear. I don't care how bad it looks. I don't care how tough it gets. You are not to fear for God says:

"Fear thou not; for I am with thee: be not dismayed; for I am thy God: I will strengthen thee; yea, I will help thee; yea I will uphold thee

with the right hand of my righteousness" (Isaiah 41:10).

He says it again *"For I the Lord thy God will hold thy right hand, saying unto thee, Fear not; I will help thee"* (Isaiah 41:13). And *"God is a very present help in the time of trouble"* (Psalm 46:1).

". . . He will make a way of escape," (1 Corinthians 10:13).

Ps. Now if you're the bully in any one of these forms, there's a special word for you in "Bully Me? . . .NO MORE." Please read the section entitled "For Bullies Only."

Action Item: Bullying began with Cain and Abel. Did you know there are many more bullies in The Holy Bible? One of those bullies was Haman. Read about him in Chapters 3 and 4 of the book of Esther. You may be surprised to see what happened to Haman, when he tried to come against Queen Esther and her people. Hint: She got the last laugh.

Do you know the story of David and Saul? When David was a very young man, he had to hide from King Saul to save his life. King Saul wanted to kill David, because he was very jealous of him.

Taking action for your protection: Read pages 52-54 of "Bully Me? ...NO MORE" on how to get dressed for battle, for all of the bullies in your life.

Bully Me...Oh NO!!!

Want to create a bully-free zone?
~ Learn to forgive. ~

"Forgive. Release! Let It Go!!"

Forgive. Release! Let it go!
Who cares how long? It's time to grow.
Hurt and shame now stand in the way of each new day.

Forgive. Release! Let it go!
Opportunity is here, if you'll open the door,
With a healthy attitude and a determined mind,
To help you endure the test of time.

Forgive. Release! Let it go!
Dare to be bold, courageous, and strong.
Plunge in with confidence,
In God put your trust.

Forgive. Release! Let it go!
It's time to live, it's your time to grow.
You deserve to be happy, and let your spirit be free

So be free from hurt, guilt and shame.

You can be free to be you and to live again.

If you'll just **Forgive, Release and let go!!**

Thought:
It doesn't matter what anyone says about you, nor what they think; if someone finds humor in the way you do things, or how you talk, stare at the clothes

you wear, or if they do mean things. Always be willing to forgive; for your willingness to forgive in any circumstance, will take you far beyond the hurt. When attitudes change through pure forgiveness, a positive atmosphere is automatically created.

Now you're walking in unconditional love, for pure forgiveness is love, unconditional. Congratulations, you've just created a "bully-free-zone."

"If you become angry, do not let your anger lead you into sin, and do not stay angry all day" (Ephes.4:26). GNT

X.
Life Changing Words
(for a better life)

Bully Me. . .Oh NO!!!

Have You Made Him Your Friend?

God hears you each time you pray. He is a personal God and loving Father. His desire is to have a personal relationship with you and a "heart-to-heart" talk every day. He wants to fill you with His power and love.

You can activate the power of God in your life as you become acquainted with Him and His Word. When you draw nigh to Him, He will fill you with His love, give you joy and peace, and cause your faith to increase.

By inviting Christ into your heart, you can have a life without extreme drama every day. And when you're faced with a challenge you can still have peace in your life when you allow the Holy Spirit to guide you or lead the way.

Have you received Jesus as Lord and Savior of your life? Let Him restore you and make your life new.

Say this out loud:
"Dear Heavenly Father, today I ask to be forgiven of sins known and unknown. I believe you sent your only begotten Son, Jesus Christ, to die for my sins, and that He was buried and arose on the third day. I believe His shed blood cleanses me from all unrighteousness, and now I am made righteous before You Father because of His blood. I accept You as my personal Lord and Savior, and right now I am born again."

You can get to know God better if you will take some time to read His Word. The more time spent reading the Bible, the less complicated your life will be. The answers to all of your problems are found there.

What a great time to receive Jesus into your heart. Now you can wake up happy, and think on good things. Expect God's favor to go before you, and plan to be a blessing everywhere you go, and expect to receive His blessings along the way.

Remember: Jesus *"is a friend that sticketh closer than a brother"* (Proverbs 18:24b); and He cares about you. He *"will never leave you nor forsake you"* (Hebrews 13:5b)

Walking in His Freedom

There is a freedom in being who God has called you to be. The Word of God says, *"Draw nigh to God and He will draw nigh to you* (James 4:8) Take time to study His Word. The more you study, the stronger you will become.

Now that you have made Him Lord of your life, you can walk in the freedom that only He can give. It means you can be free from someone else's opinion of you, free from feeling that you're not good enough, or free from feeling that you're better than someone else. You are free.

Now return to page 67 to continue on your journey toward making positive word changes in your life.

More Life Changing Words to Help You Stay Strong

"The Lord is on my side; I will not fear. What can man do unto me?" (Psalm 118:6).

"No weapon formed against me shall prosper. . ." (Isaiah 54:17a).

"If God be for us (me), who can be against us (me)?" (Romans 8:31b).

"We are (I am) more than conquerors through Him that loved us (me)" (Romans 8:37).

"God always causes us to triumph in Christ" (2 Corinthians 2:14).

"Thou will keep him in perfect peace, whose mind is stayed on thee: because he trusteth in thee" (Isaiah 26:3).

"God is our refuge and strength, a very present help in trouble" (Psalm 46:1).

"And the peace of God which passeth all understanding, shall keep your hearts and minds through Christ Jesus " (Philippians 4:7).

"Trust ye in the Lord forever, for in the Lord God is everlasting strength" (Isaiah 26:4).

Bully Me. . .Oh NO!!!

Positive Word Meanings

admirable - deserving of the highest esteem, respect, regard,
affable - gentle and gracious; pleasant to speak to; mild-mannered
amicable - loveable, friendly
astonishing - great surprise, amazement
audacious - takes bold risk, daring, brave
authentic - genuine, real, true
commendable - worthy of high praise
credible - worthy of confidence
dashing - lively, stylish, spirited
dazzling - brilliant, amazing, attractive
debonair - suave, refined, carefree
detailed - thorough, meticulous
effervescent - vivacious; high-spirited
exemplary - commendable, serving as a model, worthy of imitation
indispensable - absolutely necessary; essential
keen - marked by intellectual quickness and acuity.
laudable - deserving commendation; praiseworthy
level - rational and balanced; sensible
melodic - pleasing melody
meritorious - deserving of praise or reward
placid - Undisturbed by tumult or disorder; calm or quiet; satisfied.
receptive - capable of receiving
refined - elegant, polite
reflective - characterized by quiet thought
resolute - firm in purpose or belief; steadfast

Bully Me...Oh NO!!!

reverent - one who exhibits respect
sedate - serenely deliberate, composed; dignified in character or manner
seemly - one who conforms to standards of conduct and good taste; of pleasing appearance
selective - one who chooses carefully
self-assured - having or showing confidence, poise
shrewd - characterized by a keen awareness; artful and crafty; smart
steadfast - fixed or unchanging; steady
stunning - impressive, strikingly attractive appearance, sensational
superb - of unusually high quality; of excellence
vigilant - keenly alert or heedful of trouble or danger, as others are sleeping or unsuspicious
virtue - moral excellence, goodness
vivacious - high spirited; animated; lively

You haven't lived, until you've started living on the positive side of life. And you haven't begun to live victoriously until you've learned how to use positive word choices over the negative ones you hear.

Today is your day to walk victoriously, for you are a winner. Live victoriously positive, and be positively victorious every day. ☺

Definitions. The Free Dictionary by Farlex
Defined words taken from Positive Personality Adjectives @www.englishclub.com

"It's in the Attitude"

One person, with determination, can change the environment around them. But in order to change the conditions of the world, **we,** collectively, must change our hearts, our mindsets, and our attitudes. When **we** change, together, we can change the world.

Bully Me. . .Oh NO!!!

TEEN Strategy and Review Questions
Post Test

All throughout this resource we have provided options and shared different strategies to help you counter the negative effects of bully activity. In this section we encourage you to develop your own personal strategy, or plan of action to counter the bully attacks in your life.

This is a plan that will work any, and every time, but you'll need to practice until you have the confidence to carry it out. So let's begin by putting it on paper first. And remember, someone greater than you is fighting on your behalf, and He is always available.

1. Name those responsible adults in your life that will be there for you, to listen to your concerns, and help you take appropriate action on important matters. You can get them to help you develop a strategy to counter any adversity or bully activity in your life.

2. Change your approach to life. Wake up every day with a spirit of gratefulness and give thanks. Start with the little things. What are you thankful for?

3. Review the words on page(s) 67-68. Build your

inner spirit daily with these encouraging words. Say them out loud.

4. Take a close look at your special gifts or talents. How can you use them to make a positive difference in the world and leave a lasting impression for the betterment of others.

5. Develop a written plan for your future.
   a. Begin with a 3 month plan
   b. Next, work on a 6 month plan
   c. What is your 1 year plan?
   d. Develop a 5 year plan

6. Follow that plan. Review your plan often. Revise and update as needed. Stay on task.

7. What steps can you take to show support for someone who has been bullied?

8. Memorize the Bully-Free Pledge

9. Review the Bully Tips and practice daily

10. What happens when you smile on the inside?

11. As a guest in your parents' home, what do your they need from you? Hint: Honor, love, respect.

12. You are branding yourself with your behavior every day. How do you represent?

13. Before you make any major decision, what are

some questions you might ask?

14. Decide to have a wonderful life, and live it with great expectation. The sky is the limit.

15. Decide today, to do something to make your community, your neighborhood, your city a better place. What positive changes will you make?

16. Always remember the Golden Rule: "Do unto others as you would have them do unto you."

You must "love you" first, in order for others to see you as lovable. :)

(Pre-test is found on page 34-35).

More Anti-Bully Resources, Websites and Organizations

www.ucantbullyme.com

www.Leep4Joy.com

www.Jaredstory.com

Bully Police.org

Stopbullying.gov

Bullycide, by Brenda High

Bully Me...Oh NO!!!

Showing That You Care:

If you can save the life of one child by sharing this book, would you do it?

Too many lives have already been lost, because parents and children were not informed. Let's become proactive about bully prevention. Let's work together to preserve our future generations.

Maybe you know a child, or teenager that could benefit from the information provided in this manual. Give this book as a gift to a family in the neighborhood, at church, or at your child's school; or share it with a niece, nephew, or a friend's son or daughter. By sharing this information you will help preserve the sanctity of life.

If you picked up this book out of curiosity, we encourage you to share it. Buy an extra copy for someone else's child or consider giving this book away, just because you care.

More books by Patrice Lee:

"...Overcome Every Obstacle . . . and Land on Top"
"Bully Me? . . .NO MORE! ! !"
"Bully Me?. . .NO MAS! ! !" (Spanish Translation)
"Happy to be Me!"

Bully Me. . .Oh NO!!!

To order additional books go to:

www.amazon.com

Also inquire at your local bookstores. If the local store in your area doesn't have it visible, please ask for it. If it isn't available yet, ask them to contact us. Your inquiry may help save another child's life from the negative effects of being bullied or the fears associated with it.

Patrice Lee continues to write and publish books. She speaks to corporations, church youth groups, at conferences, and seminars; and facilitates workshops for elementary, middle and high school students, parent organizations and loving grandparents raising grandchildren.

If this book has helped you in any way, please share it with us. We would be happy to receive your comments at: ucantbullyme@gmail.com

www.ucantbullyme.com

About the Author:

Patrice Lee experienced bullying in the workplace, however, she entered the workplace every day with a smile, a positive attitude and a willingness to do and be her best.

In her books, she shares the key ingredients needed to avoid the negative effects of bullying at school, at home, at work. She desires to see families "happy, healthy and bully-free."

Leep4Joy Books and Resources help parents create that bully-free-zone for their children. You'll find encouraging words of faith, hope and love in every book.

www.ingramcontent.com/pod-product-compliance
Lightning Source LLC
Chambersburg PA
CBHW050600300426
44112CB00013B/2001